Before Christ and After Covid Influencers

Women's bodies have been curated into an idealised form since the first Paleolithic European Venus figurines Cerca 25000 years ago. In studying feminine trends and ideals throughout history it is plainly visible that the pressures Women face today are not distant from that of even our furthest ancestors.

I've collated female iconography spanning the Paleolithic Venus figures, Jōmon period Japanese dogū and the Mexican Cihuateteo amongst others. To show body ideals through time. Blending them with feminine objects from The 21st century.

This work is both a celebration of feminine power, While also critiquing toxic ideology and social constructs.

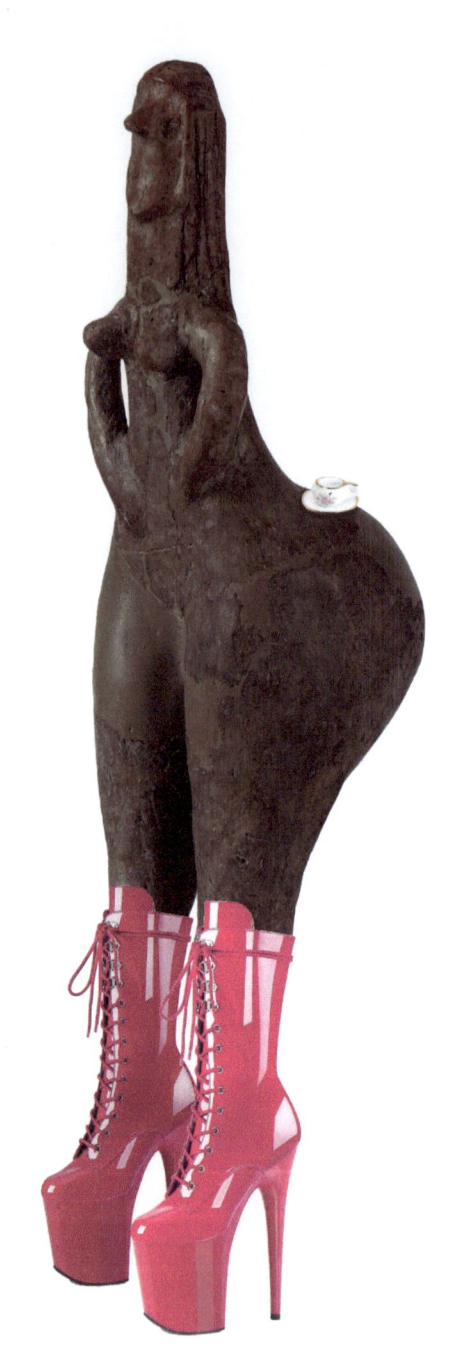

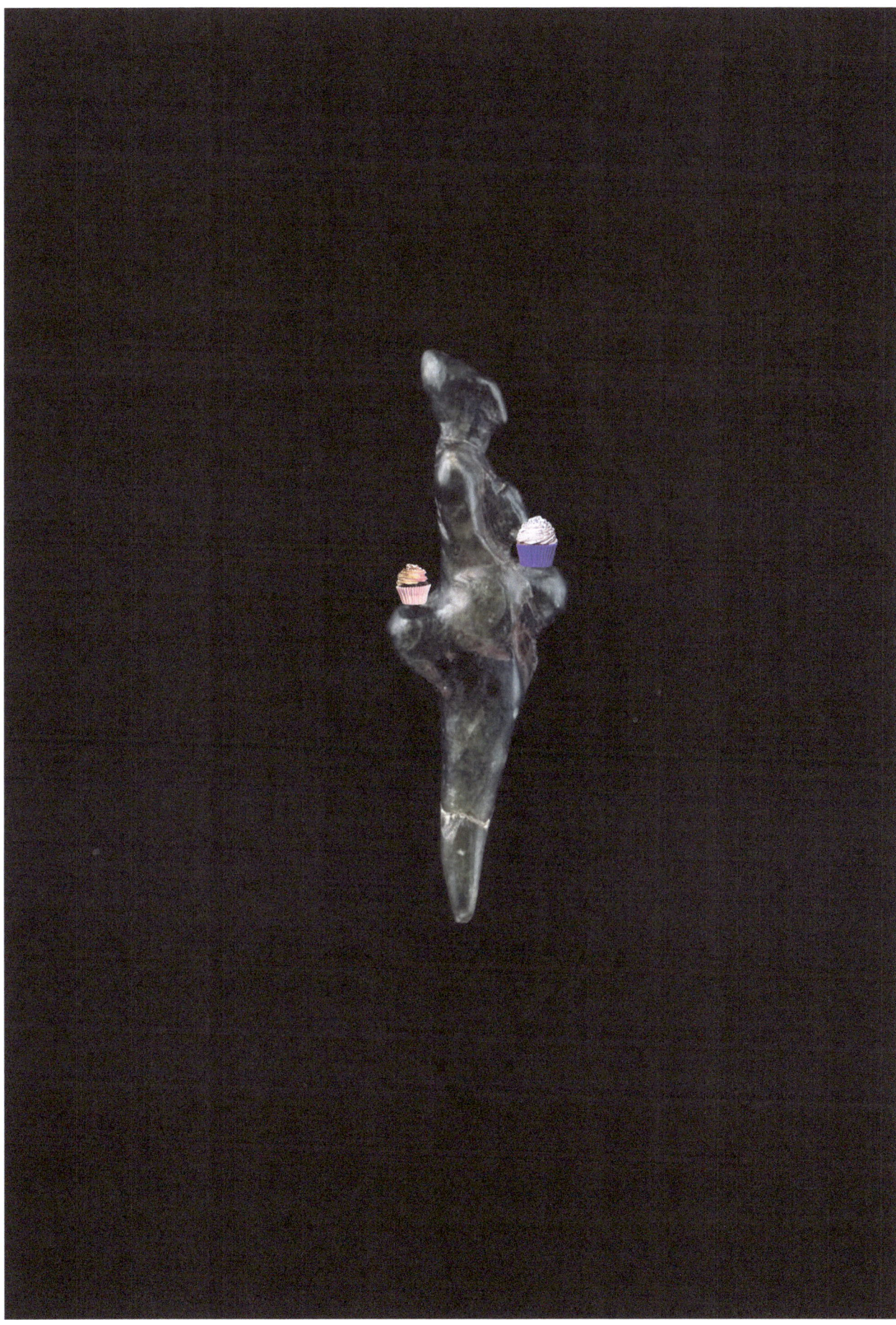

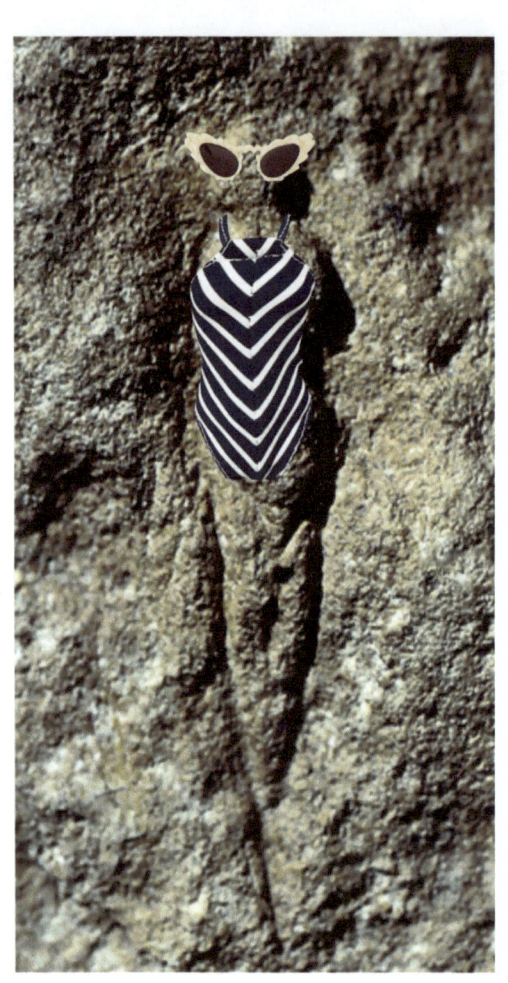

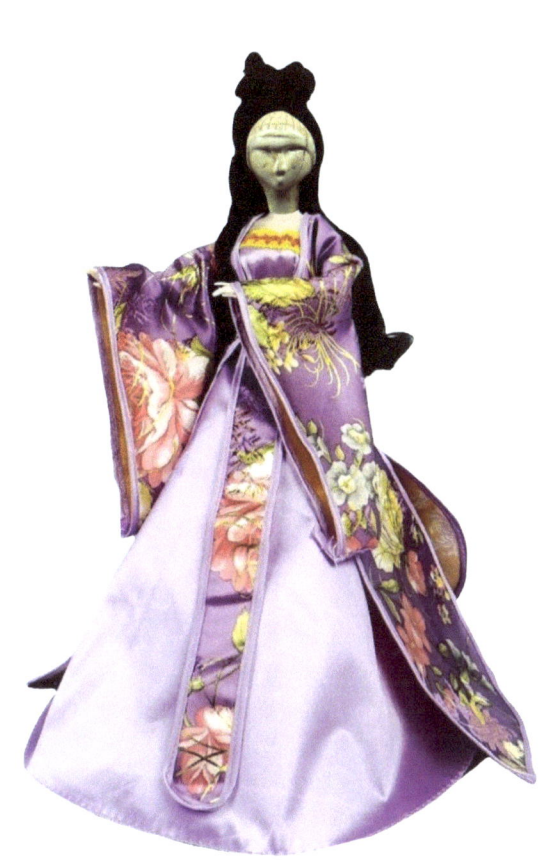

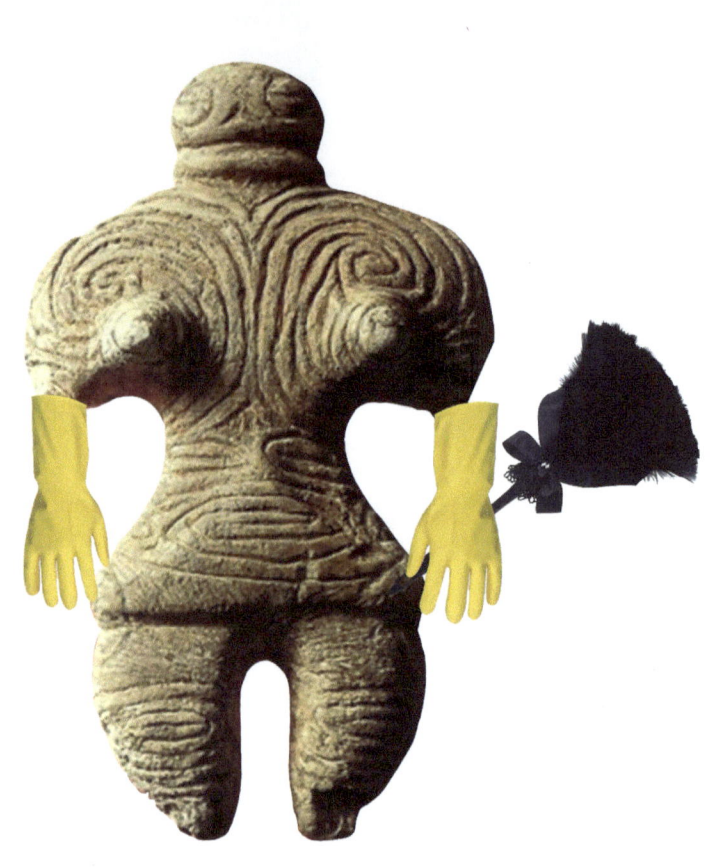

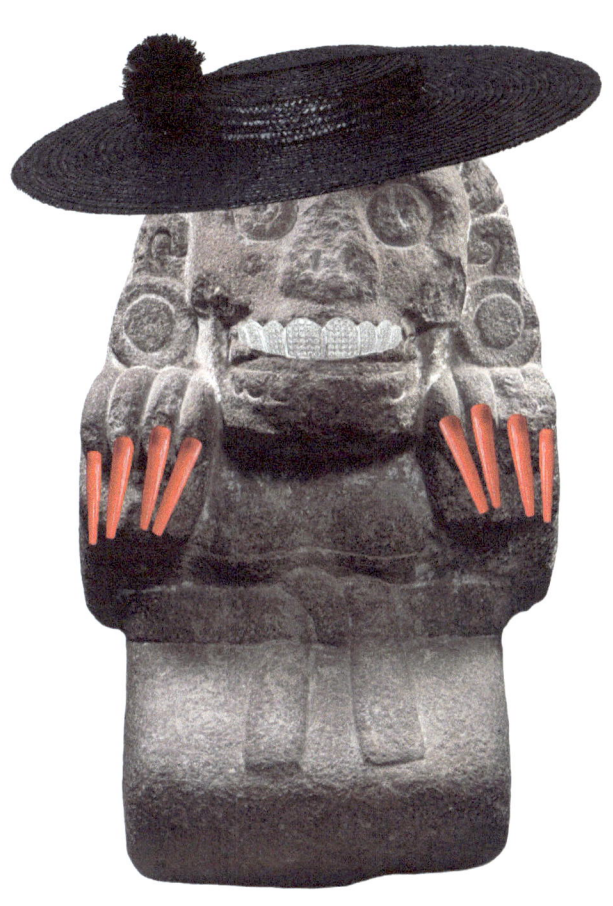

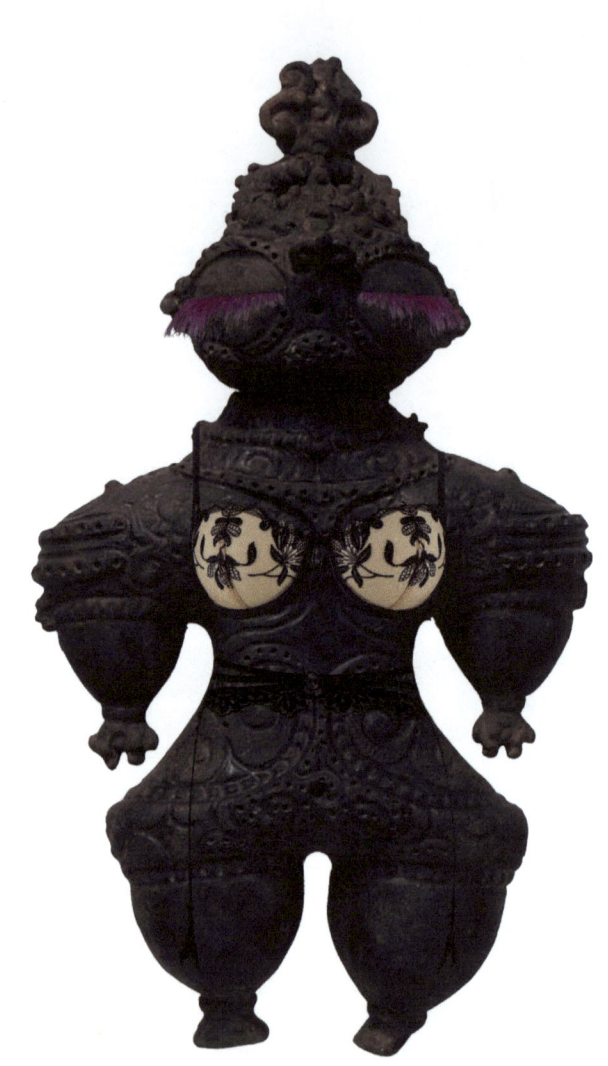

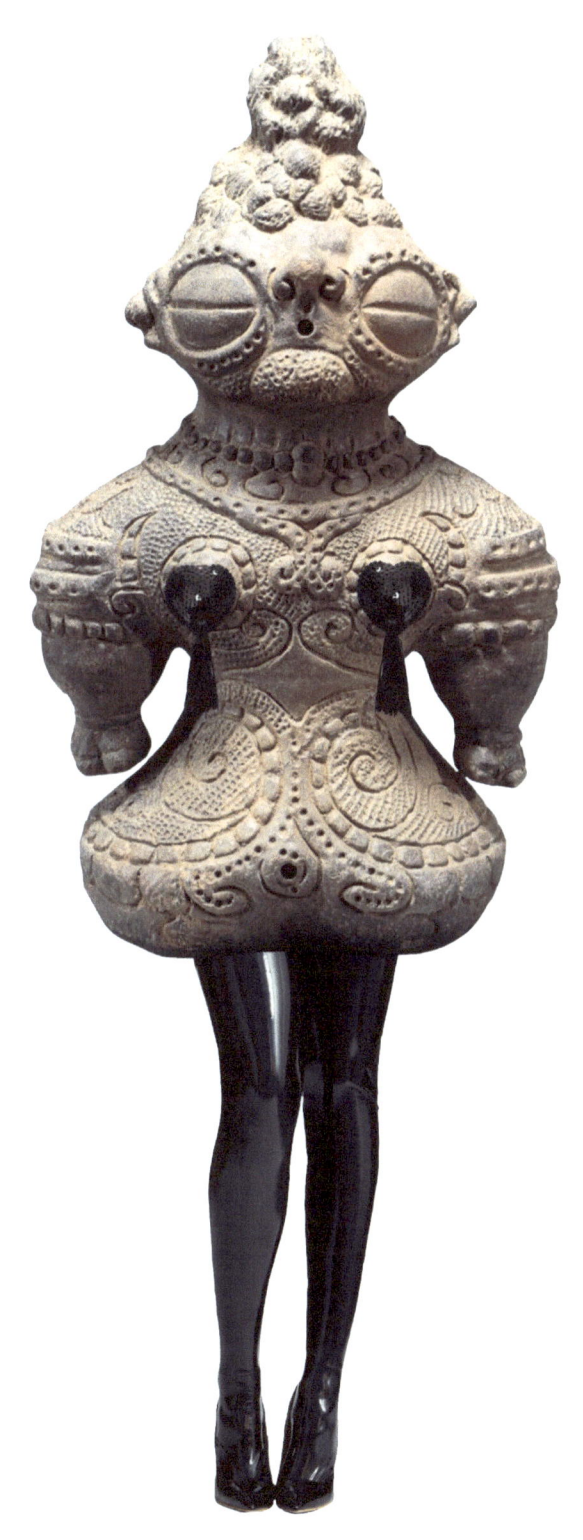

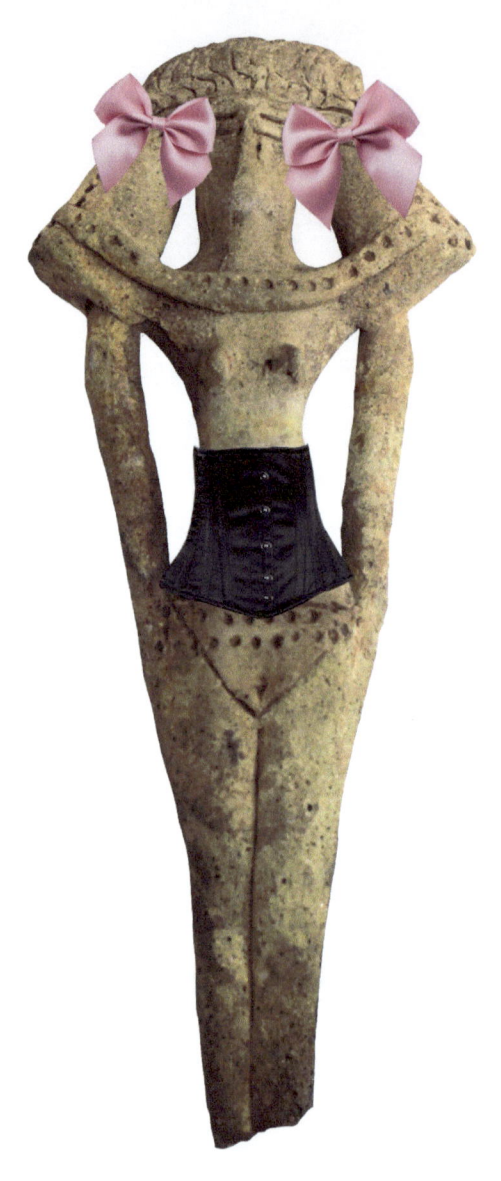

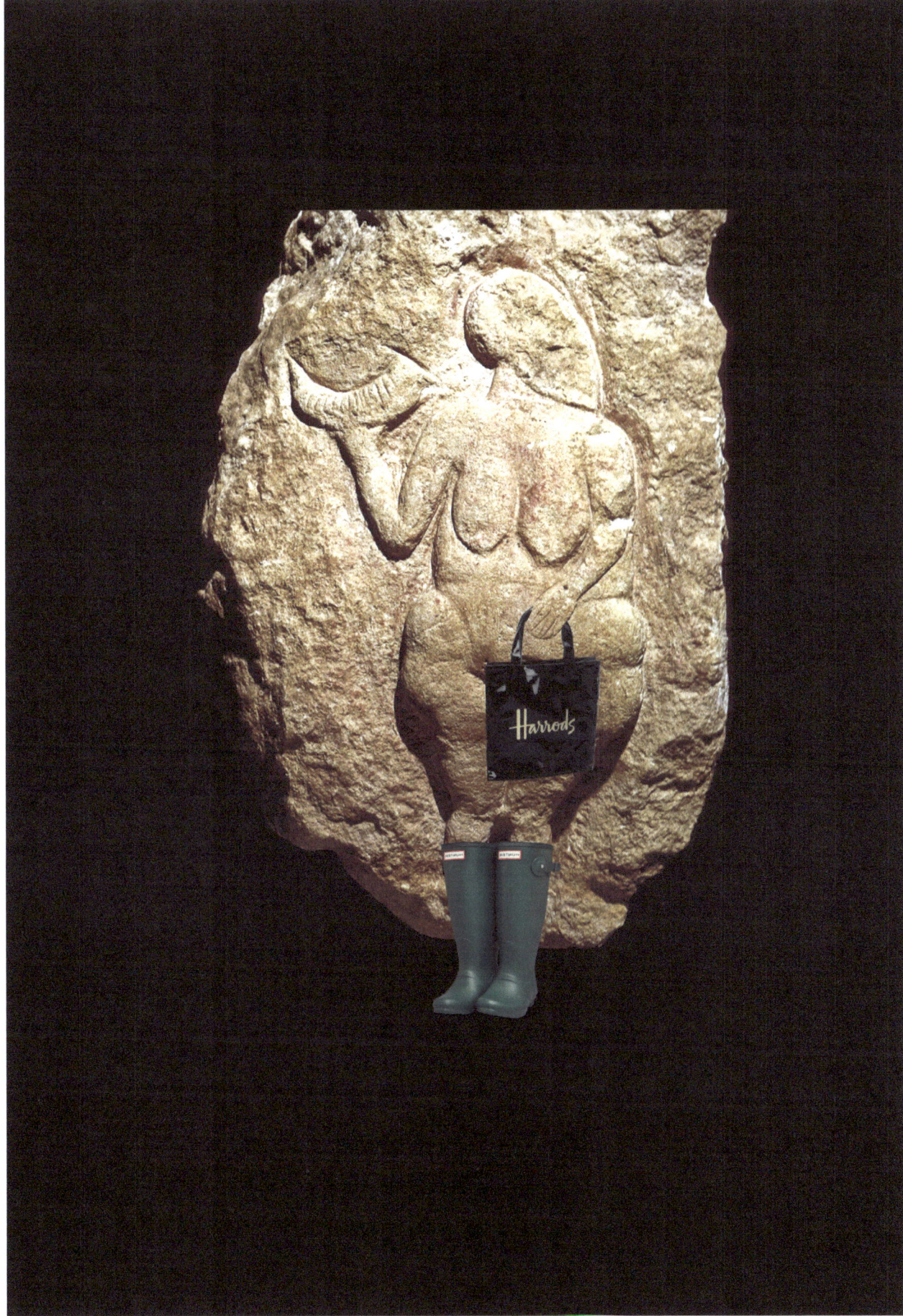

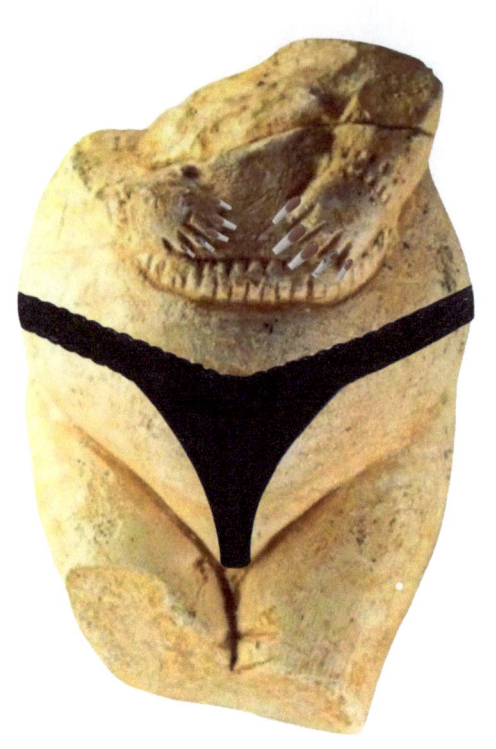

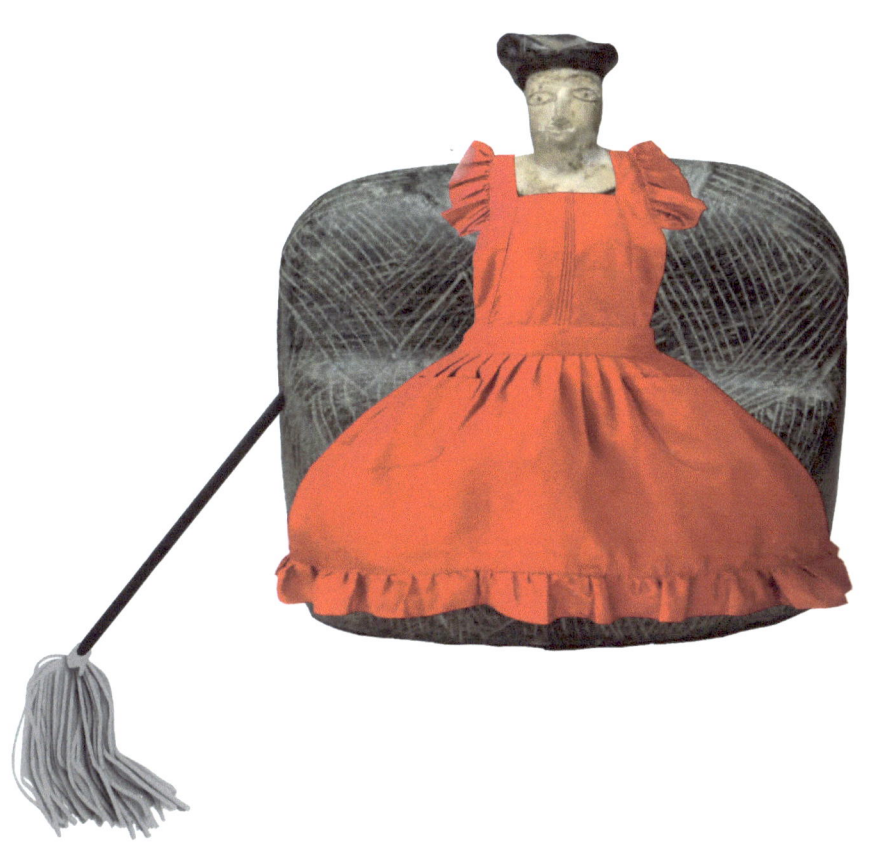

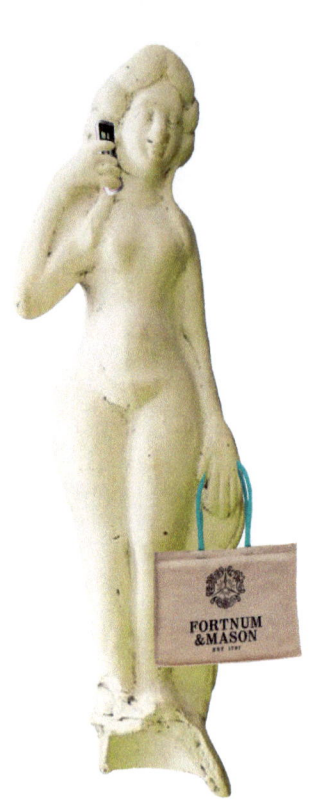

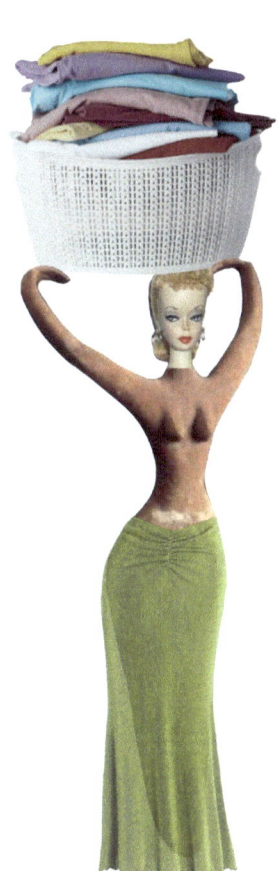

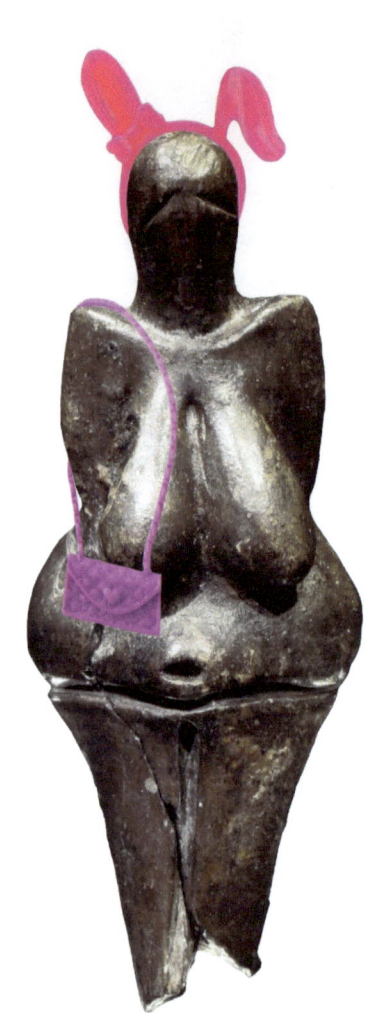

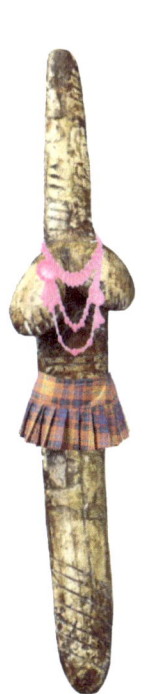

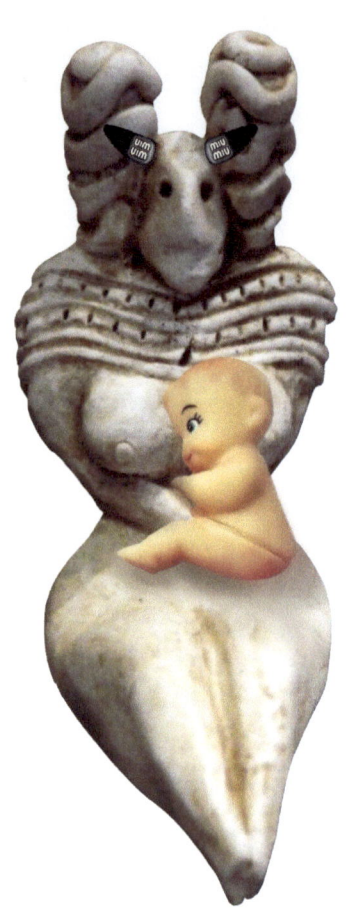

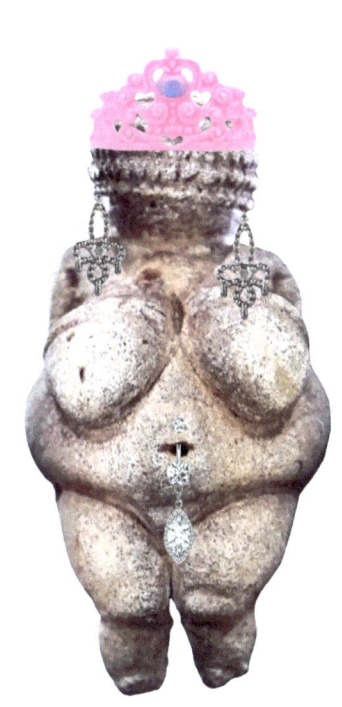

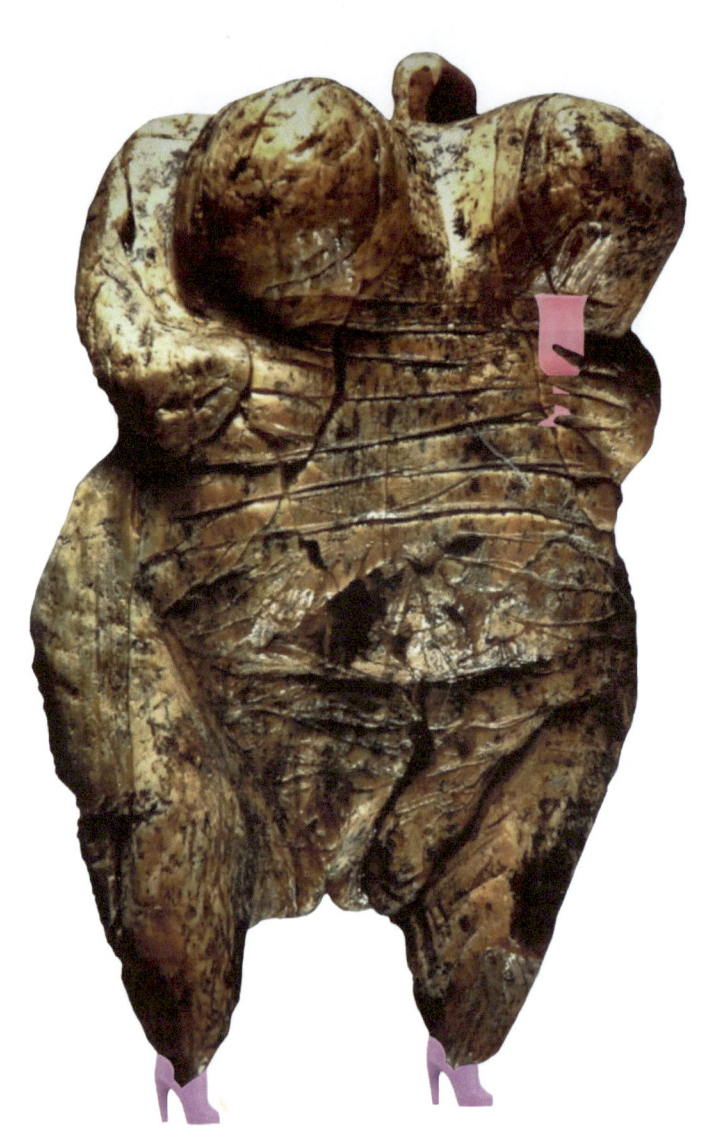

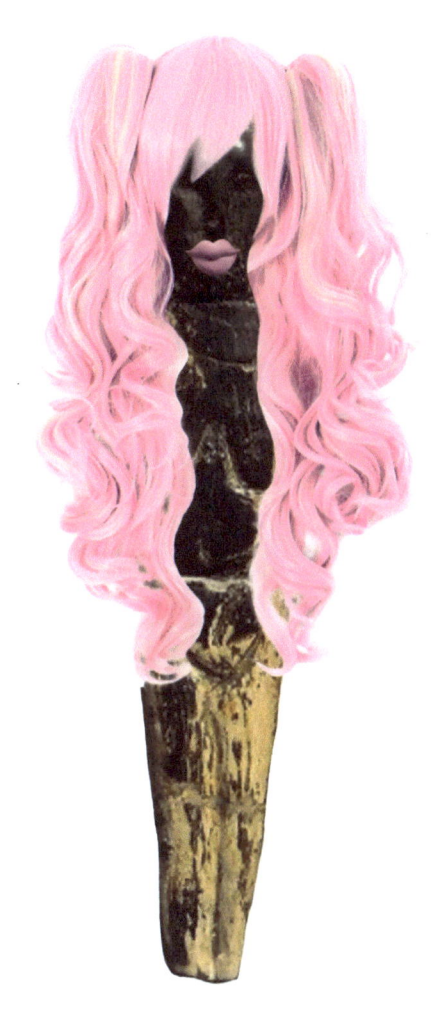

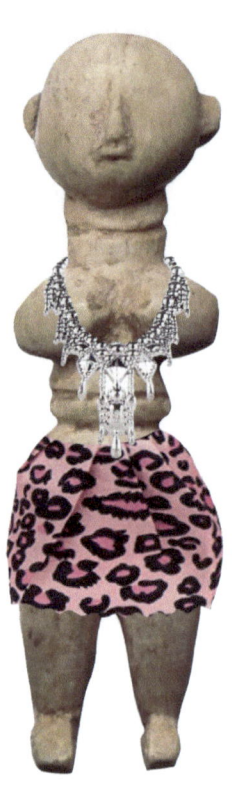

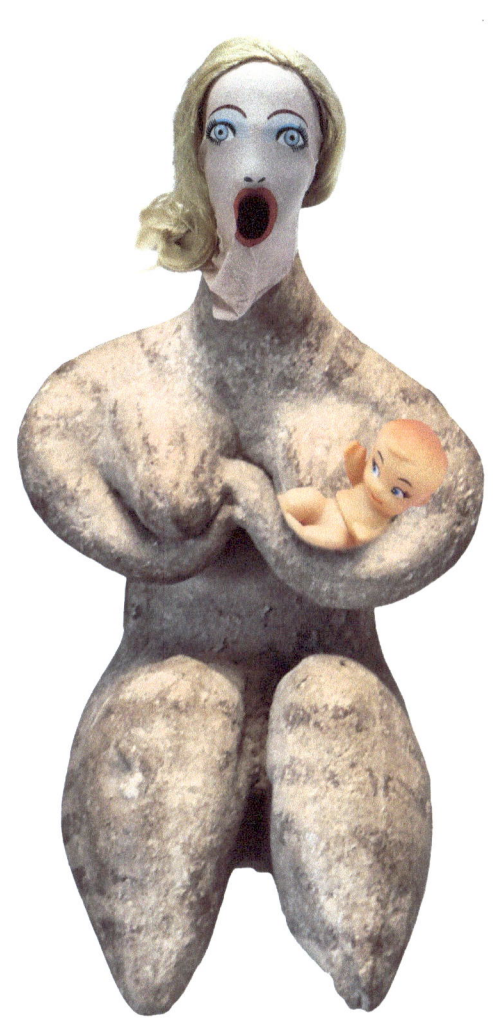

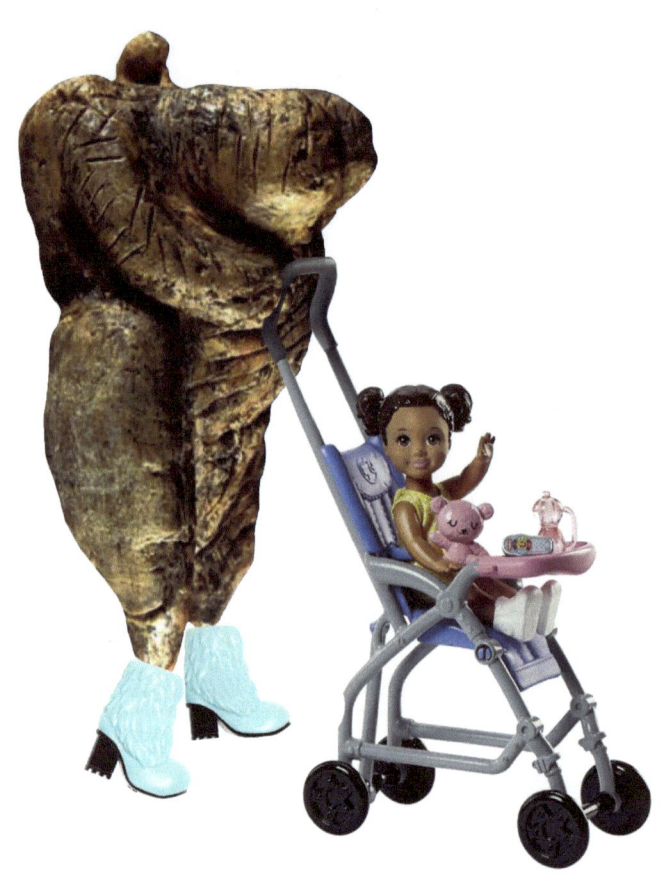

www.ingramcontent.com/pod-product-compliance
Lightning Source LLC
Chambersburg PA
CBHW040058250526
45473CB00044B/2379